The Gunpowder Plot

Contents

Written by Ciaran Murtagh

Collins

1 Introduction

It's just after midnight, 5th November 1605, and a young man is hiding in a cellar under the **House of Lords** with 36 barrels of gunpowder.

His aim is to kill the king, James I, and blow up **parliament**. What happens next will set the course of English history for over 200 years.

His name is Guy Fawkes.

But how did he get there? Why did he want to blow up the king? And did he get away with it?

To answer these questions, let's go back to 1534 when another king, called Henry VIII, had just founded the Church of England.

Henry VIII

2 Henry VIII

In 1534, England had been a **Catholic** country for nearly 1,000 years.

However, during the early 1530s, Henry VIII fell out with Pope Clement VII, head of the Catholic Church.

Henry VIII

Pope Clement VII

Henry wanted to find a new wife. To do that, the Pope had to **annul** his marriage to Catherine of Aragon. When the Pope refused, Henry VIII created the Church of England and made himself its leader. Now, he could divorce Catherine.

Catherine of Aragon

Many Catholics in England changed their religion too, but some were not happy with what Henry VIII was doing. They wanted things to go back to the way they were.

How do you think Catholics felt about changing their religion because the king wanted a new wife? Were they right to be unhappy?

3 Hard times for Catholics

Throughout the reigns of Henry VIII and later his daughter Elizabeth I, life became more difficult for Catholics in England.

Catholics were fined for not attending Church of England services. It became harder for Catholics to hold positions of power and they had to worship in secret.

Catholics hoped that Mary, Queen of Scots, a Catholic cousin of Elizabeth I, might take the throne and change things back, but in 1587, she was **executed** by Elizabeth to stop that happening.

After the Spanish Armada in 1588, when Spain (a Catholic country) tried to attack England, Catholics were viewed as enemies of the state by many.

Was this view justified? How do you think it made Catholics feel?

Elizabeth I

Mary, Queen of Scots

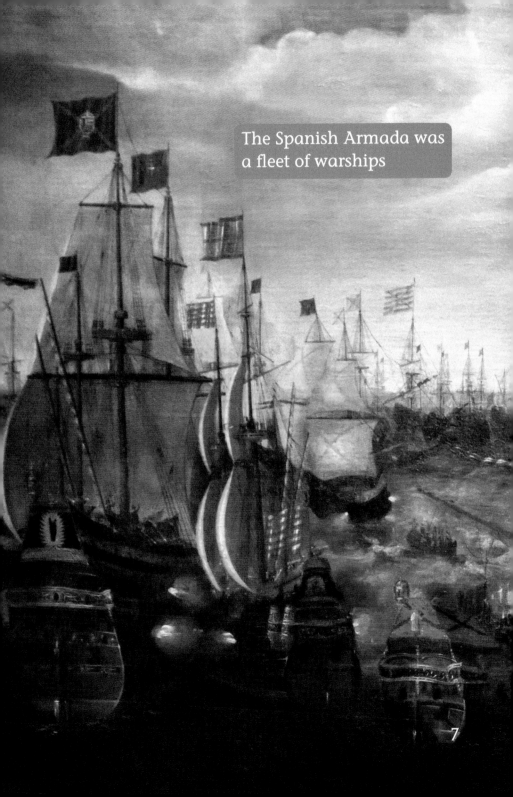

The Spanish Armada was a fleet of warships

4 The reign of James I

In 1603, after Elizabeth's death, James I became king. He was the son of Mary, Queen of Scots and had been King of Scotland since 1567, so it was hoped that James would relax some of the strict rules affecting Catholics.

However, plots by Catholics to kidnap James I were uncovered, and the rules became even tougher.

In April 1604, a **bill** was put before parliament to outlaw all followers of the Catholic Church in England.

What do you think the options were for Catholics under James I? How could they stop what was happening to them?

King James I of England
1603–1625

King James IV of Scotland
1567–1625

James I

9

5 Creating change

Robert Catesby, a member of an important Catholic family, decided to try to change the ruler by blowing up the House of Lords at the **State Opening of Parliament** and killing the king.

Was there another way he could have tried to change things? Could he have made people listen without killing anyone?

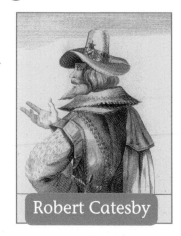

Robert Catesby

The plotters planned to blow up the House of Lords.

10

Nowadays, what are the different ways we can try and peacefully change the way we are governed?

- Vote – we can vote to change who rules us.
- Protest – we can protest on the streets and call for change.
- Petition – we can sign petitions to try and make the government think differently about an issue.

In 1604, these options weren't always available. Do you think this means Catesby was right to consider killing the king?

11

6 Meet the plotters

Catesby knew that plotting to kill the king was wrong, but he believed it was for the greater good. He started to look for other people that agreed with him and could help.

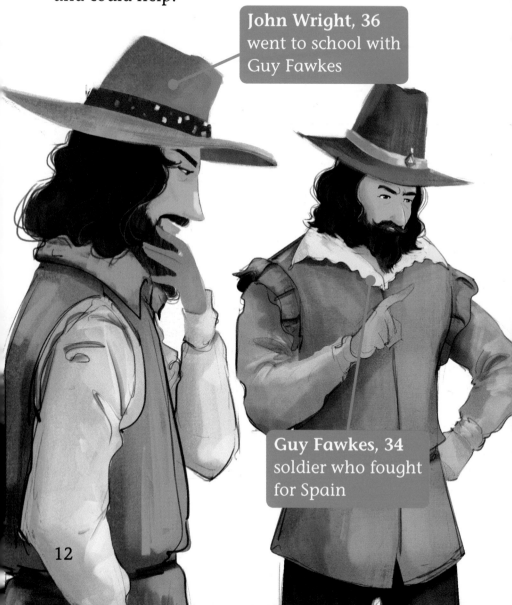

John Wright, 36 went to school with Guy Fawkes

Guy Fawkes, 34 soldier who fought for Spain

The first meeting of the plotters took place in London on 20th May 1604. The plotters all wanted to get rid of the king, but they had different reasons for doing so.

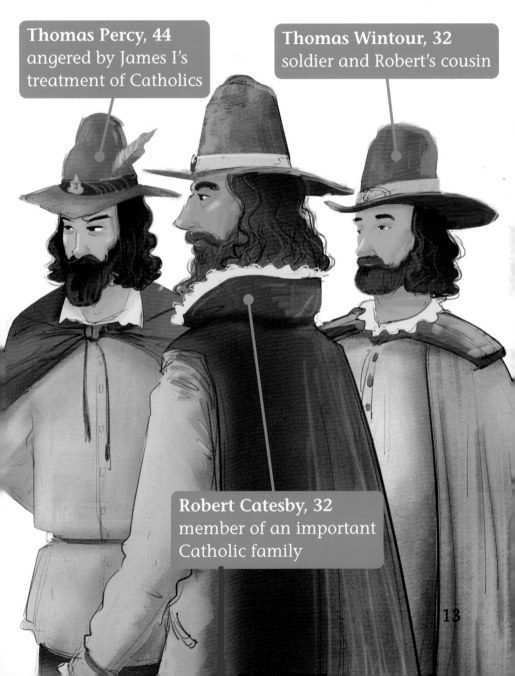

Thomas Percy, 44
angered by James I's treatment of Catholics

Thomas Wintour, 32
soldier and Robert's cousin

Robert Catesby, 32
member of an important Catholic family

7 A plan is formed

In a private room at *The Duck and Drake*, the five plotters agreed to remove James I from the throne.

They didn't have a complete plan, but they started to share ideas.

Thomas Percy was worried their ideas would come to nothing, saying: "Shall we always gentlemen, talk and never do anything?" But Robert Catesby reassured him that this plot would be a success.

At the end of the meeting, the plotters swore on a prayer book, promising to keep the meeting and their plot a secret.

Over the next few months, the plotters began to work on their plan.

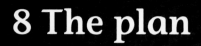

8 The plan

There were two parts to their plan.

1. To blow up the Houses of Parliament with gunpowder while James I was there.

What do you think this might have meant for the country? What reaction would there be to the plot succeeding?

2. To kidnap the king's daughter, Elizabeth, keep her safe and make her queen once James I was dead.

Elizabeth was nine years old at the time. The plotters planned to bring her up as Catholic and marry her to a Catholic husband.

Now you know the plan, do you think it will succeed? What could go wrong?

Elizabeth

9 The countdown

June 1604: Thomas Percy rents a house in Westminster, close to the Houses of Parliament. He pretends that Guy Fawkes is his servant.

*Guy Fawkes used the name John Johnson as an **alias** to make sure he wasn't found out.*

October 1604: Robert Catesby's home is used to store gunpowder and supplies. Robert's house was opposite the Houses of Parliament. The plotters planned to row the barrels of gunpowder across the river Thames and hide them in a cellar.

March 1605: Thomas Percy rents a cellar under the Houses of Parliament.

July 1605: The gunpowder has been hidden in the cellar, ready for the State Opening of Parliament and the plotters gather at Catesby's house in Lambeth.

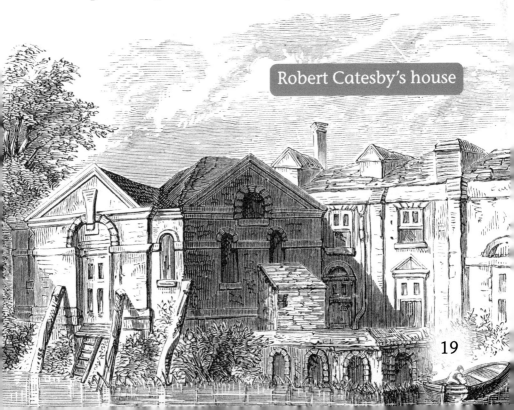

Robert Catesby's house

10 The date is set

At the same time, Robert Catesby travelled the country, speaking to people he thought might help him with his plans.

By November 1605, there were 13 plotters in the gang.

Everything was ready; the plotters just needed James I to visit parliament. Unfortunately, a **plague** (known as the Black Death) was spreading in London, and the State Opening of Parliament was delayed twice.

But on 28th July, it was announced that the State Opening would take place on 5th November 1605.

The plotters had their date.

✼ORDERS,

thought meete by his Ma-
ieſtie, and his Priuie Counſell, to be
executed throughout the Counties of this
Realme, in ſuch Townes, Villages, and other
places, as are, or may be hereafter infected with the Plague, for the
ſtay of further increaſe
of the ſame.

Alſo, an Aduiſe ſet downe by the beſt
learned in Phyſicke within this Realme,
containing ſundry good Rules and eaſie Medi-
cines, without charge to the meaner ſort of people,
aſwel for the preſeruation of his good Sub-
iects from the plague before Infecti-
on, as for the curing and orde-
ring of them after they
ſhalbe infected.

G. 896.

¶ *Imprinted at London by* ROBERT
BARKER, Printer to the Kings
moſt Excellent Maieſtie.

ANNO 1603.

> Plague Order delaying the opening of parliament

21

11 The Monteagle letter

Lord Monteagle was a Catholic nobleman who would have attended the State Opening of Parliament.

On 16th October 1605, he received an **anonymous** letter warning him not to go.

It said: "… they shall receive a terrible blow this parliament and yet they shall not see who hurts them …"

Lord Monteagle passed the letter to Robert Cecil, the king's most important minister. Robert showed it to the king.

The king realised that the words "terrible blow" might be talking about an explosion, and decided to try and catch the plotters.

Nobody knows for sure who wrote the letter.
It's thought it was a plotter who was also a friend of Lord Monteagle who didn't want him to be killed.

Would this have been an easy letter for the plotter to write? Did they do the right thing?

12 4th November

Even though the plotters knew they had been found out, they decided to go ahead with their plan. Do you think that was a good idea? What could they have done instead?

This was their plan: on 4th November, Guy Fawkes would wait in the cellar under parliament until the king arrived for the State Opening the next day, then set off the 36 barrels of gunpowder that had been stored there.

Guy Fawkes's hiding place

He and six of the plotters would then flee London by boat.

Once the king was dead, Everard Digby, the last plotter to join the gang, would ride to Coombe Abbey in Warwickshire to kidnap the king's daughter, Elizabeth.

13 Capture!

However, the Monteagle letter had done the trick and the king ordered a search of the Houses of Parliament.

During the first search, soldiers found someone, now thought to be Guy Fawkes, but didn't think he was a threat.

A second search was ordered and just after midnight on 5th November, Guy Fawkes and the gunpowder were found.

Guy was captured.

Elizabeth was moved to the nearby city of Coventry. She was safe too.

The plan had failed.

Guy Fawkes's lantern

Guy Fawkes is captured under the Houses of Parliament.

14 On the run!

Guy Fawkes was taken to the Tower of London to be questioned.

The remaining plotters left in London fled.
They went north to the Midlands, desperate to escape capture and find support. At Dunchurch, they met Everard Digby.

the Tower of London

Robert Catesby was determined to make his plot a success. He lied to Everard, telling him that the king was dead and that they should continue the fight. Everard joined the plotters and **raided** nearby Warwick Castle for supplies.

Warwick Castle

They travelled to Huddington to try and gain support from friends and family.

Word had spread about what had happened, and the plotters were turned away wherever they went.

They ended up in Holbeche House near Dudley, tired and without support.

What do you think they did next?

Holbeche House

15 The confession

Meanwhile in London, Guy Fawkes was being questioned. He gave his name as "John Johnson" and wouldn't name any of the others involved.

The king used **torture** to try and make Guy tell the truth. By 8th November, 3 days after being captured, Guy had confessed and named the other plotters.

Guy Fawkes's signatures before and after being tortured

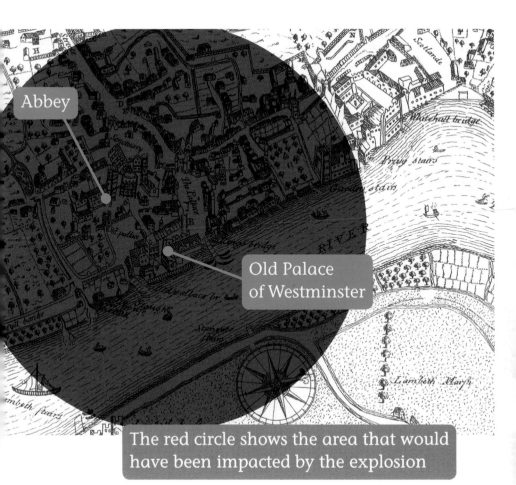

Abbey

Old Palace
of Westminster

The red circle shows the area that would
have been impacted by the explosion

In 2005, to mark the 400th anniversary of the plot,
a television programme recreated the Gunpowder
Plot to see what would happen if Guy Fawkes had
been successful.

It found that everyone within 100 metres of
the barrels would have been killed and the Houses of
Parliament destroyed.

16 The last stand

At Holbeche House, the plotters knew they were running out of time to think of what to do with the gunpowder.

Their supplies of gunpowder had got wet, and they tried to dry it out in front of the fire. A spark lit the gunpowder and it exploded.

Robert Catesby was burnt and another plotter was blinded.

On 8th November, the **Sheriff** of Worcestershire attacked Holbeche House.

In the attack, Catesby, Wright and Percy were killed. Thomas Wintour was shot in the shoulder and arrested.

The five men who had met in *The Duck and Drake* were now either dead or in prison.

The Sheriff of Worcestershire and his men attack Holbeche House.

17 Put to death

Over the next weeks, the other plotters were found and imprisoned.

People who had known the plotters were also questioned.

On 27th January 1606, the eight plotters still alive were brought to trial at the Star Chamber.

The Star Chamber was a court in the Palace of Westminster named after the stars on its ceiling.

the Star Chamber

The men were sentenced to death.

On 30th January, Everard Digby was executed in front of crowds in St Paul's Churchyard.

On 31st January, Thomas Wintour and Guy Fawkes were executed.

In a final act of defiance, Guy jumped from the gallows, breaking his own neck, before the executioner was ready.

18 A day to remember

The Gunpowder Plot made things even harder for Catholics in England.

New laws were passed that stopped Catholics voting in elections. They couldn't become **officers** in the navy or army. They weren't allowed to be **lawyers**.

Catholics weren't allowed to vote in elections until 1829.

These rules lasted for over 200 years. It was only in 1829 that some Catholics were given the right to vote.

Do you think this was fair punishment for what Guy and the other plotters tried to do?

Afterwards, James I tried to reunite the country. He wanted people to celebrate the fact he had foiled the plan.

In 1606, the Thanksgiving Act was passed. It called for an annual celebration to give thanks for the failure of the Gunpowder Plot.

James I signs the Thanksgiving Act.

19 Bonfire Night

Every year between 1606 and 1819, special services were held on 5th November and church bells were rung to remember the Gunpowder Plot, in accordance with the Thanksgiving Act.

In the UK, people still commemorate 5th November. It's often known as Bonfire Night. Large bonfires are lit and fireworks are set off to remember the explosive end the plotters wanted for James I.

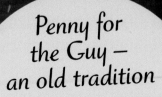

Penny for the Guy – an old tradition

A dummy of Guy Fawkes is made and stuffed with straw. The guy is wheeled around by children, then burnt on the fire.

Children celebrating Bonfire Night, 1970

The biggest 5th November celebration takes place in Lewes, Sussex, England. Bonfire societies organise six different bonfires in and around the town.

Before the bonfires, members of the societies march through the town setting off fireworks.

Up to 5,000 people take part in the celebrations with over 80,000 people gathering to watch.

Large **effigies** are burnt on the bonfires. Nowadays, the effigies are of political figures or celebrities that have been in the news.

In the town of Ottery St Mary in Devon, England, Bonfire Night is celebrated by racing flaming barrels through the street – don't try this at home!

41

20 Guy Fawkes and protest

While the Gunpowder Plot happened over 400 years ago, it changed English society for many years to come.

For centuries, Guy Fawkes was condemned for trying to blow up parliament. Nowadays, people sometimes remember him as someone who fought for freedom.

Did you know?

To this day, as a tradition, the cellars in the Houses of Parliament are checked for gunpowder before the State Opening of Parliament. None has ever been found again.

Officials still check the Houses of Parliament for explosives.

Sometimes people wear masks of Guy Fawkes's face when protesting.

He was even included in a list of the 100 Greatest Britons of all time.

How do you think Guy Fawkes and the rest of the plotters are best remembered? As criminals who tried to kill the king, or as heroes trying to achieve freedom and equality for Catholics?

Glossary

alias a false name

annul to cancel by law

anonymous made by someone unknown

bill a document that makes law

Catholic a religion – a branch of Christianity

effigies creations that have a likeness of a person

executed to be killed by the state

House of Lords one of the Houses of Parliament in England

lawyers people trained in the law

officers high ranking officials

parliament where rules and laws are made

plague an infectious disease that can be deadly

raided stole or took something, after forcing your way into somewhere

sheriff someone who enforces the law

State Opening of Parliament an annual ceremony where the king or queen formally opens parliament

torture causing pain over a period of time to force someone to give information

Index

A timeline

March 1603
*James I becomes
King of England*

May 1604
*Plotters meet for
the first time at
The Duck and Drake*

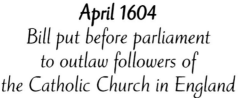

April 1604
*Bill put before parliament
to outlaw followers of
the Catholic Church in England*

July 1605
*Gunpowder hidden
under the Houses of
Parliament; date for
State Opening of
Parliament set*

October 1605
*Monteagle letter
received and passed
to the king*

January 1606
*The surviving
plotters are tried
and executed*

November 1605
*The Gunpowder Plot
is foiled. Guy Fawkes
is caught*

Where do you think it started to go wrong for the plotters?

Is there a key turning point that meant their plan was doomed to failure?

What do you think would be different about the world we live in today if they had succeeded?

Ideas for reading

Written by Christine Whitney
Primary Literacy Consultant

Reading objectives:
- be introduced to non-fiction books that are structured in different ways
- listen to, discuss and express views about non-fiction
- retrieve and record information from non-fiction
- discuss and clarify the meanings of words

Spoken language objectives:
- participate in discussion
- speculate, hypothesise, imagine and explore ideas through talk
- ask relevant questions

Curriculum links: History: Develop an awareness of the past; Writing: Write for different purposes

Word count: 2628

Interest words: House of Lords, parliament, Catholic, annul

Resources: paper, pencils and crayons

Build a context for reading

- Ask children to share their experiences of fireworks. Have they seen any? If so, where was this and on what occasion?
- Encourage children to look closely at the front cover of the book. Ask for a volunteer to explain what is happening and who the characters might be.
- Read the blurb on the back cover and ask the group to suggest answers to the question: *Why did a group of men want to blow up parliament?*

Understand and apply reading strategies

- Read Chapters 1 and 2, checking children's understanding of the *House of Lords*, *parliament* and *Catholic*.
- Continue to read Chapters 3 and 4 together. Ask children to explain how Catholics must have felt when *a bill was put before parliament to outlaw all followers of the Catholic Church in England.*
- Read on, pausing at the end of Chapter 8. On page 14 it says, *Over the next few months, the plotters began to work on their plan.* Ask children to explain this plan.